EUGENIO PUCCI

ALL VENICE

IN 205 COLOUR PHOTOGRAPHS

BONECHI EDIZIONI « IL TURISMO »
FIRENZE

FOUNDATIONS RESTING ON PILES: ARCHITECTURAL FEATURE OF VENETIAN BUILDINGS

In the fifth century, the inhabitants of the northern Adriatic coast took flight before the barbarian tribes sweeping down over Italy and decided to settle the lagoon islands—this is the origin of the city later to be known as Venice. The first problem that had to be faced was constructing dwellings that would be safe from the frequent floodings the area was subject to, and this problem was probably overcome by the use of tree-trunk piles. Thereafter, as the buildings became more and more complex structures, stone and brick replaced wood as the main building material. Nevertheless, it was impossible to avoid the use of piles and still today the foundations of Venetian buildings rise upon millions of piles sunk into the muddy depths of the lagoon. Architectural marvels such as the Basilica of San Marco, the Rialto Bridge, and the Belltower required hundreds of thousands of these piles to sustain them - a truly incredible engineering feat. Thus we can say that Venice actually rests upon a forest of tree-trunks, mostly larchwood (This wood is fortunately quite rugged and highly resistant to the action of water.)

On the left, a cross-section of the Belltower of San Marco and the Loggetta. Below, a detail of the foundation of the Belltower showing the sizes of the weight-bearing piles and the various strata of earth.

The drawings have been reproduced by courtesy of the Direction of the Doges' Palace - Venice.

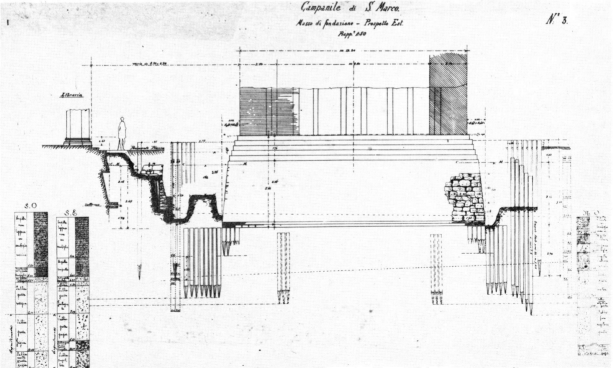

VENICE

The color photos on this and the following pages are meant to give you an idea of what Venice, a city that really needs no introduction, is like. The city's fame rests not only on its unique lagoon setting amidst a web of charming canals, which in itself is quite unusual, but also on the countless masterpieces of art and architecture which in Venice have their own distinctive language and style.

The city is of course anchored to its rich historical past which began with the decline of the Holy Roman Empire of the West and the resulting barbarian invasions. The hordes who swept down over Italy bringing death and destruction to the mainland towns caused their inhabitants to flee and seek refuge on the numerous islands and islets dotting the lagoon. In fact, the first settlements in what is now the Rialto area were the result of the tenacity of the refugees from Aquileia, Altinum, and Padua, who not only dug an intricate web of canals, but also reinforced the land on which they raised their buildings.

This incredible undertaking, carried out according to what today would be judged as an intelligent townplanning scheme, included excavation of the Grand Canal and the numerous minor canals (called "*rii*") that crisscross the city and connect the 118 islets on which the city rises (pedestrians can cross more than 400 bridges to get over the canals and *rii*).

A sweeping view of the docks of St. Mark's. Starting from the left we see: the domes of the Church of Santa Maria della Salute dominating the Punta della Dogana, the green island of the Royal Gardens, and then Sansovino's Library, the Doges' Palace, the Belltower of St. Mark's, and, finally, the Riva degli Schiavoni.

In order to build on the territory it was necessary to reinforce the ground surface with huge treetrunks which were used as pylon supports. The structures that rose on the new foundations, palaces, churches, and public buildings, are proof of the power and the glory achieved by the Venetians in their sea trade and territorial conquests. To defend what they had conquered, the Venetians did not always have to resort to military actions, for they were famous world over for their skill as diplomats and ambassadors.

The city which has grown up over the centuries is a tribute to the intelligence and tenacity of human endeavor. It is a city which has to be seen to be believed—words cannot describe it, nor do justice to its uniqueness. Only by wandering around its picturesque *campi, campielli* (Venetian words for squares), *calli* (alleyways), and *rii* can you really get to know and appreciate what people have always considered one of the wonders of the world.

And it is not just the city's unique setting, as we said before, which makes Venice so special. Celebrated artists added to and enhanced its natural beauty by adorning it with tiny and huge masterpieces of art and architecture, painting and sculpture, while others enlivened its atmosphere with great music and theater. In fact, Venice is a must for scholars and art lovers from every corner

of the globe who cannot claim to know the cultural and artistic history of Italy until they are familiar with Venice's.

Seeing the palaces along the Grand Canal and the remarkable buildings dotting the city's various quarters (known, in Venice, as *sestieri*) allows the sightseer and art lover to get an historical prospective on the growth and development of the city. As our gondola or vaporetto (water bus) carries us along the waterways, Romanesque, Gothic, Flamboyant Gothic, Renaissance, and Baroque buildings pass before our eyes, living illustrations of every style and period. Venice is a blend of all of them, no style or period has been passed over. Perhaps, though, the most incredible impression we are left with is the profusion of masterpieces of the so-called minor arts which here led to the development of a solid tradition in every craft, from mosaic-making to glassblowing, traditions that have continued strong and flourishing to this very day.

All this is not only to be found along the Grand Canal, it exists everywhere. There is no corner of Venice which has not been touched by the magic wand of creative genius. This is indeed mind-boggling if you consider how huge a territory Venice actually covers: 7,061 square kilometers for the city proper and 13,700 if you include the Marine Terminal and the islands.

Arrival in Venice – Venice can be reached by car, train, or ship. If you come by car, you must cross the Ponte della Libertà built in 1933 alongside the railroad. The road ends at the Piazzale Roma which serves as both a parking lot and bus terminal for the buses linking the city with the mainland. A *vaporetto* (water bus) goes from the **Fondamenta di Santa Croce** to St. Mark's Square in about half an hour. Or else, you can take a gondola or motorboat.

This is a view of the **Santa Lucia Railroad Station** named after the church which originally stood on this site dedicated to St. Lucy. The bridge which connects it to the mainland, erected in 1846, rests on 75,000 pylons sunk into the lagoon—a remarkable engineering feat.

Upon leaving the modern station, we find ourselves right before the Grand Canal and the vaporettos and gondolas which carry passengers to downtown Venice.

THE GRAND CANAL

This is the most famous of the Venetian canals. An upside down "S" which bisects the whole city, the canal is almost 2 1/2 miles long, approximately 15 feet deep, and ranges from about 100 to 225 feet across.

A gondola ride is, of course, the best way to enjoy the Grand Canal. It is an unforgettable experience to smoothly glide past lovely palaces and buildings, charming canals and *rii,* and beneath picturesque bridges. Whatever the season, Venice is magical, each moment has its particular charm. Whether you have come here to be stirred by memories of history, art, literature, or music, or else simply to enjoy the emotional experience of the scenery and setting, Venice will not disappoint you. Its ever-changing setting, constantly altered by sun, clouds, rain, and sea, creates an almost fairytale atmosphere, enchanting and unreal at the same time, that no other city in the world is able to duplicate.

Opposite the station is the **church of San Simeone and Giuda** with its distinctive weathered copper dome and imposing porch with Corinthian columns. Although originally founded in the ninth century, the building we see today was erected by Giovanni Scalfarotto between 1718 and 1738. The circular-plan interior was inspired by the Pantheon in Rome.

The Bridge of the Scalzi – This is the first bridge we encounter on our way to St. Mark's Square. Originally of iron, it was rebuilt in 1933 after a design by E. Miozzi.

The fine **church of Santa Maria di Nazareth** or **Santa Maria degli Scalzi** was designed by Baldassarre Longhena and erected between 1660 and 1689. The intricate façade, designed by Giuseppe Sardi, is a noteworthy example of the Venetian Baroque, inspired by Classical motifs. Inside is the tomb of the last doge of Venice, Lodovico Manin.

First built in the 11th century, the picturesque **church of San Geremia** (photo above) was completely remodeled in the 1700s. The Romanesque belltower is one of the oldest in Venice. The mortal remains of a matyr, St. Lucy of Syracuse, are preserved inside the church. On the right side of the church is Palazzo Labia, a fine 16th century palace, and on the left the Palazzo Flangini designed by Giuseppe Sardi in the 17th century.

On the right is the **Fondaco dei Turchi (Turkish Storehouse).** Originally headquarters for the Oriental merchants stationed in Venice, this building recalls the Venetian Byzantine style of the thirteenth century, and especially that of the Doges' Palace.

The Ca' Pesaro (Photo on the left) – This impressive Baroque palace is the masterpiece of its architect Baldassarre Longhena who erected it between 1679 and 1710. Two important museums are inside: the Oriental Museum and the International Gallery of Modern Art.

Photo above: opposite the Ca' Pesaro is a row of magnificent Venetian-style palaces. Starting from the left: the 17th century **Palazzo Ruoda,** the 16th century **Palazzo Gussoni Grimani della Vida** (attributed to Michele Sanmicheli), and three 17th century palaces, the **Palazzo da Lezze,** the **Palazzo Boldù,** and the **Palazzo Contarini-Pisani.**

The Ca' d'Oro – This is one of the finest examples of 15th century Venetian architecture. Its name (Ca' d'Oro = Golden House) derives from the gilding which once adorned the entire façade. Bartolomeo Bon and Matteo Raverti were commissioned by the nobleman Marin Contarini to design the palace which was erected between 1421 and 1440. Its last owner, Baron Giorgio Franchetti, bequeathed it together with the magnificent art collection decorating its rooms, to the Italian state in 1916. On the facing page is a view of the courtyard.

THE FRANCHETTI GALLERY

The Franchetti Gallery is inside the Ca' d'Oro, overlooking the Grand Canal. The collection includes paintings and furnishings from different periods. Nevertheless, none of the works or rooms bear identification plates in accordance with Baron Franchetti's wish that it retain the appearance of a collection in a private home rather than take on the anonymous look of a state museum. Beneath the arcade on the ground floor is a collection of antique statuary from various places, whereas on the upper floor there is a painting gallery hung with famous masterpieces, such as Carpaccio's Annunciation and Death of the Virgin which once belonged to a cycle (now scattered) from the Scuola degli Albanesi. There is also a group of Flemish school paintings, con-

In the photo above: *View of the docks and the Punta della Dogana* by Francesco Guardi who, along with his contemporary Canaletto, is one of the most celebrated 18th century landscapists. On the right: *Sleeping Venus with Cupid* by Paris Bordone, one of Titian's best known followers, active in the first half of the 16th century.

sidered one of the finest collections of Flemish art in Italy, and of course outstanding Italian masters such as Titian (Venus at the Mirror), Giovanni Bellini (Virgin of the Lovely Eyes), and Gentile Bellini (Portrait of Mohammad II, commissioned by the Republic in 1479 in Constantinople). Recently, several rooms of the adjoining Palazzo Giusti have been annexed to the Ca' d'Oro.

In the photo above: The *Piazzetta di San Marco*, another painting by Francesco Guardi revealing the artist's incredible technical mastery and skillful handling of light and color. Guardi trained under both his brother, Gian Antonio, and the great painter, Giovan Battista Tiepolo. On the right: the *Allegory of Wealth*. This painting is a typical example of the Mannerist style in vogue in 16th century Florence where it was painted.

Photo above: The brick structure on the right is the **Pescheria** (fish market). Although there has been a fish market on this spot since the fourteenth century, this building dates from 1907. Designed by Laurenti and Rupolo, it is an imitation of the 15th century Venetian Gothic style. On the opposite side of the canal we can make out in the background the **Palazzo Michiel dalle Colonne** with its distinctive ground floor colonnade.

Photo below: the **Fabbriche Nuove di Rialto,** designed by Jacopo Tatti, better known as Sansovino, in 1555, is now the Courthouse of Venice.

The Fabbriche Vecchie di Rialto, photo above, was designed in the early 1500s by Scarpagnino. Today it is the site of the city fruit and vegetable market.

Photo below: the **Fondaco dei Tedeschi** (German Storehouse) received its name from its occupants, German merchants, who assembled here to carry on trade with the Orient. Designed by Scarpagnino in 1508, the building is now the main Post Office. Along the Rio del Fondaco are several other fine typically Venetian-style palaces.

The Rialto Bridge – Although great architects such as Michelangelo and Palladio took part in the competition for the construction of this bridge, Antonio da Ponte was awarded the commission by the Venetian Republic.

The bridge was built between 1588 and 1591 with a single span and without the shops which were added on later. The structure is 156 feet long, 72 feet wide, and 24 feet tall. From the Ponte di Rialto you get a magnificent view of the Grand Canal, with the Riva del Carbon (Coal Bank) and the Riva del Vin (Wine Bank).

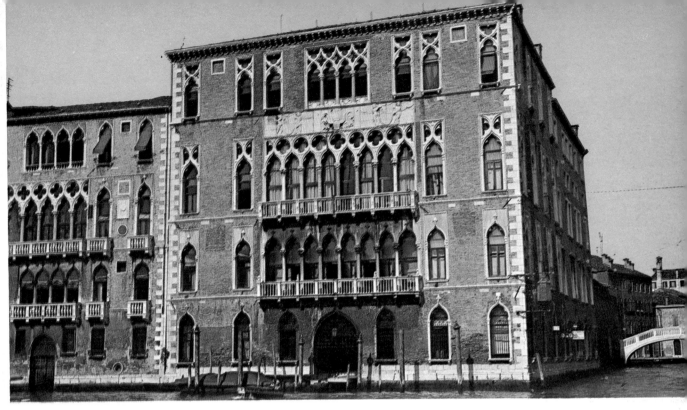

The Ca' Foscari (Photo Above) – One of the finest of the buildings designed in the Venetian Gothic style, the palace is now the Business School and Economics Department of the University of Venice. It was commissioned by Doge Francesco Foscari, who ruled the Republic of Venice for over thirty years.

The Grassi Palace (Photo below) – The 18th century Classical style palace was designed by Giuseppe Massari and commissioned by the Grassi family, originally from Bologna, who became part of the Venetian nobility in 1718.

The Ca' Rezzonico and the Academy Bridge – This lovely Baroque palace was designed by Baldassarre Longhena in the 17th century, although the upper storey was added on in the 18th century by Giorgio Massari. The Ponte dell'Accademia, a single span wooden bridge built in 1932, leads to the Academy Gallery, featuring one of the finest collections of Venetian painting in the world. The museum and gallery will be described separately.

THE MUSEUM OF 18TH CENTURY VENICE

The Museum of 18th Century Venice – It is inside the Palazzo Rezzonico on the Grand Canal. The palace, originally belonging to a noble Venetian family, Rezzonico, was the last home of Robert Browning (the room where he died in 1889 has been left as it was). The City of Venice purchased it in 1935 and used it for the reconstruction of the interior of an 18th century patrician dwelling, furnishing it with superb period pieces, vases, and wall hangings. In addition, it is filled with valuable paintings by Carriera, the Tiepolos, and Longhi. The Salone da Ballo (Ballroom) on the second floor is breathtaking for its size, grandiosity, and stupendous inlaid furniture. One of the best reconstructions is the so-called Villa dei Tiepolo which consists of the grisaille frescoes painted in 1753 by Gian Domenico Tiepolo (son of Giovan Battista) for his family estate in Zianigo on the Brenta River.

In the photo above, a room in the Museum of 18th Century Venice. Below, a 17th century Flemish tapestry depicting *Solomon and the Queen of Sheba*. On the following page: the *Spinner* by Pietro Longhi.

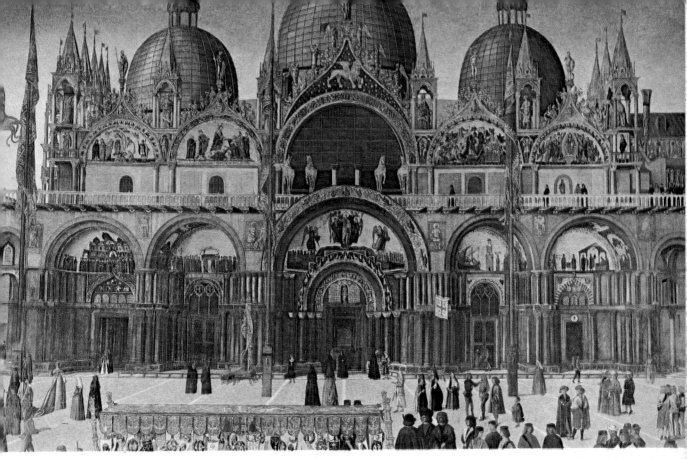

THE ACADEMY GALLERIES

Five hundred years of Venetian art are on exhibit in the Accademia, a museum which cannot be equalled anywhere for homogeneity, clarity of exposition, and quality. Its origins go back to 1750 when the Republic of St. Mark's decided to endow the city with an "Accademia di pittori e scultori" (Academy of Painters and Sculptors) under the direction of Piazzetta. The original Academy occupied the "Fondachetto delle Farine" (Flour Storehouse). In 1756 the Academy was granted official recognition and Piazzetta, by then an old man, decided to leave it in the capable hands of Giovan Battista Tiepolo who created the core of a first group of works by the pupils of the Academy. In 1807, it was decided to transfer the art school and the works displayed in it to a more fitting place and the choice fell upon the Scuola and Church of the Carità (in the Campo della Carità). The collection considerably expanded as numerous works from suppressed churches and monasteries poured in.

In the above photo, a detail of Gentile Bellini's *Procession in Piazza San Marco;* on the right: the *Madonna degli Alberelli,* by Giovanni Bellini.

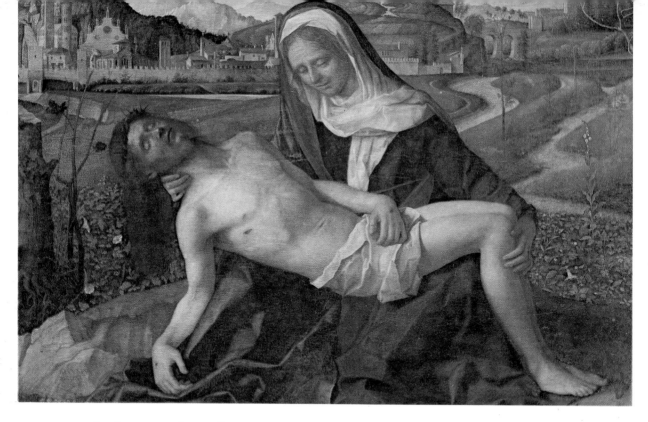

In the upper photo, *Pietà* by Giovanni Bellini. On the lower left, the *Madonna della Misericordia* by Jacobello del Fiore; on the right, the *Mystic Marriage of St. Catherine* by Lorenzo Veneziano.

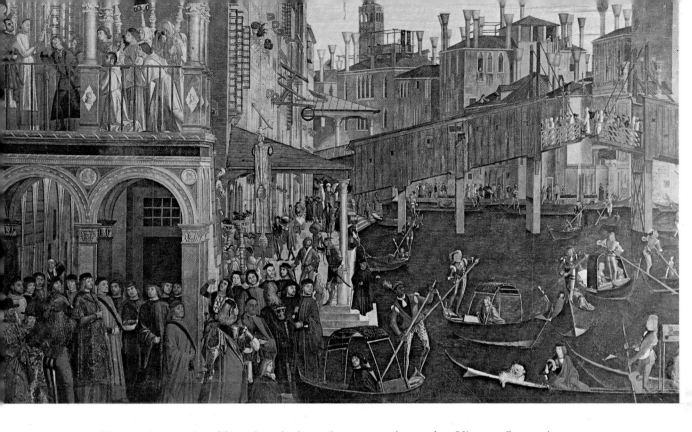

Photo above, the *Miraculous healing of a possessed man* by Vittore Carpaccio; below, two details from the *Story of St. Ursula* cycle, both by Vittore Carpaccio.

In the upper left photo: the *Arrival of the Ambassadors* from the Story of St. Ursula by Carpaccio; below: two details from the same work. Above: the *Tempest* by Giorgione.

The Ca' Granda (Photo above) – The Palazzo Corner, nicknamed Ca' Granda (Large House) because it is so big, was designed by Sansovino in the 16th century. The striking façade is a combination of Venetian and Classical motifs. Inhabited by the rich and powerful Corner family up to the early 1900s, the palace now belongs to the Italian government and is occupied by the Prefecture and other government offices.

The Church of Santa Maria della Salute (Photo on the right) – The church, clearly visible from Piazza San Marco, is a Baroque masterpiece by Baldassarre Longhena. Over the centuries the octagonal building with its distinctive dome and curlicue brackets has inspired thousands of artists who have immortalized it in countless paintings, drawings, and engravings. Commissioned by the Venetian Senate (the decree is dated October 22, 1630), the church was erected in thanksgiving to the Virgin whose intercession ended a terrible plague that had caused over 47,000 victims.

We take one last look at Santa Maria della Salute before getting off the vaporetto or gondola since, having come to the end of the Grand Canal, we find ourselves in Piazza San Marco (St. Mark's Square). Before us is the **harbor of St. Mark's,** with the Canale della Giudecca on our right and the charming **Isle of San Giorgio Maggiore** (photo below) with Palladio's splendid church of the same name, in front of us. The waterways are heavily trafficked by vaporettos, barges, and gondolas going to and from the lagoon islands and the Lido and Venice. To our left are interesting sights such as the Arsenale (old shipyard), the site of the International Biennial of Art, and the Naval College. A walk along the canal in this direction is worthwhile.

The Piazzetta of St. Mark's – Disembarking from our vaporetto at the San Marco station, we pass a small 15th century palace in the Lombard style which is now the Port Authority Building. After passing a garden (Giardino del Palazzo Reale) and the Zecca (Mint) designed by Sansovino, we find ourselves in the square which serves as a kind of antechamber to the majestic space of Piazza San Marco. This is the so-called Piazzetta (little square) bounded on the west by a superb Renaissance building designed by Sansovino in 1535, the Libreria Marciana and on the east by the Doges' Palace, with the Basilica of San Marco on the far side. On the canal side are two tall granite columns originally from the Orient which were set up here in 1172 by Niccolò Barattieri. On the south column is a statue of St. Theodore, the first patron saint of Venice, while the lion of St. Mark's on the other column, which was also brought from the Orient, symbolizes St. Mark, the city's patron saint and the power of the Republic of Venice. The space between the two columns was once used for public executions.

ST. MARK'S SQUARE

The square is the Venetians' open-air drawing-room. Here all the major events of the city's long history were played out, here the Republic was born, flourished, and died. It is truly impressive in size: the huge trapezoid is 569 feet long, 266 feet wide on the church side, and 185 feet on the opposite side. The paving we see today, de-signed by Andrea Tirali and laid out in 1723, consists of a simple geometric pattern in marble and plain grey trachyte from the Euganean. Originally the square, known as "*morso*" (tough) because its terrain was hard-er and tougher than that of the rest of the Venetian territory, was surrounded by trees and crossed by a canal.

Piazza San Marco (Above) – On the south side is the **Procuratie Nuove,** residence of the **Procuratori** (magistrates) of St. Mark's, a Classical building designed by Vincenzo Scamozzi in 1584, on the west, the **Napoleonic Wing,** a neo-Classical building designed by Giuseppe Soli in 1807, and, on the north, the **Procuratie Vecchie,** built between 14th and 15th centuries.

THE CORRER MUSEUM

The Museo Civico Correr occupies the so-called Napoleonic or "Nuovissima" wing and the Procuratie Nuove along Piazza San Marco. It was founded in 1830 by a wealthy Venetian, Teodoro Correr, who bequeathed his fabulous art collection to his native city. The museum remained in the Palazzo Correr until 1922 when it was moved to its present site. The collection, further expanded over the years by various donations and bequests, has had to be split up into different sections: the one pertaining to 18th century Venice is displayed in Palazzo Rezzonico, whereas the archeological one is in another wing of the Procuratie Nuove (entranceway from the Piazzetta). The Museo Civico Correr now includes three separate departments: History, Paintings, and the Italian Unity Period. The Painting Gallery occupies 19 rooms on the third floor.

In the photo above, a *View of Venice* by Giuseppe Heintz; on the right, *Portrait of Doge Giovanni Mocenigo* by Gentile Bellini. On the following page, the *Courtesans* by Carpaccio.

40

The Clocktower – The pictures show the upper part of the tower where the bell is being struck by two male figures dubbed "Moors" due to the dark hues they have taken on over the four centuries that they have been sounding the hours in Venice. The figures were cast in bronze by Ambrogio de la Anchore in 1497. Beneath the top of the tower is the symbol of the city, the winged lion, and below the lion is a gilded copper statue of the Virgin and child, attributed to the 15th century sculptor-goldsmith Alessandro Leopardi. Each year, on the Feast-day of the Ascension (which comes 40 days after Easter) and during the whole week of the Ascension festivities, at the striking of every hour, figures of the three Magi preceded by an angel, go in and out of the side doors pass before the Virgin, and bow before her. On the right is a photo of the winged lion.

43

The Belltower – The soaring brick belltower is a copy of the original which was built between 888 and 912 over Roman foundations and which collapsed on July 14, 1902. The tower was then restored piece by piece and once again opened to the public on the Feast-day of St. Mark, the city's patron saint, in 1912. "Paron de casa" (master of the house), as the Venetians call it, stands over 320 feet tall, its bellchamber commanding a spectacular view of the city and the lagoon. On the top is a gilded angel weathervane.

At the foot of the tower is **Sansovino's Loggetta,** a charming Renaissance structure which the great architect erected between 1537 and 1549. The niche statues, also by Sansovino, represent Apollo, Mercury, Pax, and Minerva, symbols of the virtues that were supposed to inspire the actions of the Republic of Venice. Although the collapse of the belltower also caused the destruction of the loggia, it was painstakingly reconstructed using the original materials recovered from the rubble. The loggia originally served as the headquarters for the Guard of the Republic responsible for protecting the members of the Consiglio Maggiore when the council was in session.

ST. MARK'S BASILICA

It has been said that St. Mark's embodies the entire stream of the political, social, and religious history of the *Serenissima Repubblica di San Marco* (as the Republic of Venice was called). Its origins go back to 829 when Doge Giustiniano Partecipazio commissioned the church as a fitting place in which to preserve the mortal remains of St. Mark the Evangelist who had become the sole patron saint of the city. The building was destroyed in a fire in 827 and rebuilt as we see it today between 1043 and 1071 by order of Doge Domenico Contarini. Originally the church was a combination of Byzantine (the Greek cross plan and domed covering) and Romanesque styles. Over the centuries its unadorn walls were embellished with a glowing mantle of mosaics and precious marbles and its structure enhanced by architectural elements from the Orient. As a result, the basilica today is a harmonious blend of the Byzantine, Gothic, Renaissance, and Islamic styles. The army of craftsmen, artists, and laborers, Venetian and otherwise, who worked on it contributed to creating a true masterpiece of art and architecture.

The photo shows the façade of the basilica, almost 170 feet long, which is divided into five sections by imposing archways. The balustrade with the bronze horses over the entranceway divides the lower level from the upper level. The building is crowned by striking domes which create an unusual Oriental effect. The façade is adorned with precious marbles and mosaics. The bronze flag poles in front of the building originally flew the colors of the Republic. They were designed and executed by Alessandro Leopardi in 1505.

The Venetians carrying St. Mark's body into the church, dated 1260-1270.

The Body of St. Mark being worshipped by the Venetians by Ricci, 1728.

THE PORTAL MOSAICS

The Venetians welcoming the body of St. Mark to Venice by Vecchia, 1660.

The Removal of St. Mark's body from Alexandria in Egypt by Vecchia, 1660.

The main portal with the **Last Judgment** by L. Querena, 1836. ▶

The Deposition of Christ   **The Descent into Limbo**

THE MOSAICS OF THE SPIRES

These mosaics were designed by Maffeo da Verona and executed by A. Gaetano in 1617-1618.

The Resurrection of Christ   **The Ascension of Christ**

The main spire is a masterpice of 15th century Tuscan sculpture. The figures ▶
of St. Mark on the pinnacle and the angels were carved by the Florentine
master, Niccolò Lamberti, in the early 1500s.

On the upper storey terrace in front of the central window are four Hellenistic gilded **bronze horses,** part of the booty captured by Doge Enrico Dandolo in Constantinople during the Fourth Crusade of 1207. They were placed here in the mid 14th century, where they remained until Napoleon carried them off to Paris when Venice was occupied by the French troops in 1797. Then, in 1815, they were returned to Venice and have recently been extensively restored.

The Atrium – From the main portal we enter the Atrium with its splendid mantle of golden mosaics. Its slightly pointed arches, the earliest of their kind in Italy, support six small domes. The pavement is covered with mosaics (which create incredible effects of luminosity when the church is flooded, as it often is, in fall or winter).

The marble columns against the walls are of various origin, some are even said to have come from the Temple of Solomon in Jerusalem. The mosaics on the arches, lunette recesses, and domes illustrating scenes from both the Old and New Testaments, are all by expert 13th century Venetian craftsmen.

VQVEEDILVVIVQVADRAGITADIEB;SVPRAETQVINOECICVBITISALCIO
AQVASVPOMSMONTES;CVVCOSVPTEETOISCROSVPRAEMISNOE

TLIVENITAOEVPOASRAVOLILEIORE·ETITELLEXNOEXCESSAETO·DILVIII
·PORAMARCVINNVBIB;   ·ETERITSIGNVEEDE
                                                      TROSITVLI

·NOEOPTVLITHOLOCAVSTVDNO·   ·PIDLVVV

The Atrium of St. Mark – The photos above show episodes from the *life of Noah* and the *Deluge*. The emphasis on story-telling reaches its apex in the dramatic scene of the Deluge (above left) with the half submerged bodies being dragged into the whirlpool. Outstanding for its fresh naturalism is the scene with the animals shown freely wandering in an airy landscape (below right). All of the scenes from Genesis bear a startling resemblance to the miniatures in the Cotton Bible, an illuminated manuscript dating from the High Middle Ages.

The interior of St. Mark's – The sumptuous Byzantine interior dates from the time of Doge Contarini. In the form of a Greek cross, it is aisleless and has a raised choir. The columns of the transept aisles sustain the so-called *ma tronei*, or women's galleries, while the domes are supported by square pillars. The first version of the basilica had no marble or mosaic decoration. The elaborate decoration we see today was added in 1159 with materials brought back from the Orient and Dalmatia. The profusion of gold and gilding has given the church the nickname of

55

the "golden basilica." The columns and capitals are worth careful viewing for they are proof of the incredible level of skill reached by the Byzantine craftsmen who carved them between the 3rd and 13th centuries. Noteworthy as well is the marble pavement of geometric and animal motifs which dates from the 12th century. By the imposing altar screen before the choir is a block of veined marble which the Venetians used to refer to as the "sea" due to its wave-like patterns.

The mosaics inside the basilica – The church's special charm is mostly a result of the incredible wealth of mosaics covering every bit of wall and ceiling space inside the building (they actually cover an area of over 4000 square meters). The earliest mosaics date from the time of Doge Domenico Selvo who ruled the Republic between 1071 and 1084. The second, or Byzantine period, lasted from the 12th through the 13th centuries and was the time of maximum splendor for the Venetian school which had begun to flourish at the end of the 11th century when it was still influenced to a great extent by the mosaic school of Ravenna. By the 12th century the Venetian craftsmen had developed a form of artistic expression all their own and artists and craftsmen flocked from all over to work in the Venetian studios. The development of the art of the mosaic went hand in hand with the development of Romanesque architecture during the 12th and 13th centuries. In the 14th century mosaics began to get their inspiration from painting, although a real decline does not

Christ's entry into Jerusalem

Christ enthroned

Christ in the Garden of Gethsemane

appear until the Renaissance period when painting supplanted mosaics as the most widespread means of expression. The *Procuratori* made a valient attempt to rekindle interest in mosaics by calling in famous artists such as Paolo Uccello and Andrea del Castagno, both from Florence, to design cartoons for mosaics. This led to period of renewed interest during the 16th century when renowned masters such as Titian, Lorenzo Lotto, Tintoretto, Veronese, Piazzetta, Salviati, and Bassano produced cartoons which were transformed into superb mosaics.

The Miracle of St. Mark

St. John the Evangelist

St. Mark the Evangelist

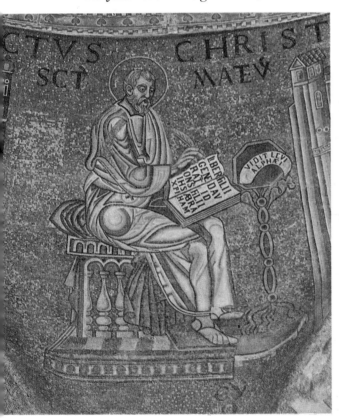

St. Matthew the Evangelist

St. Luke the Evangelist

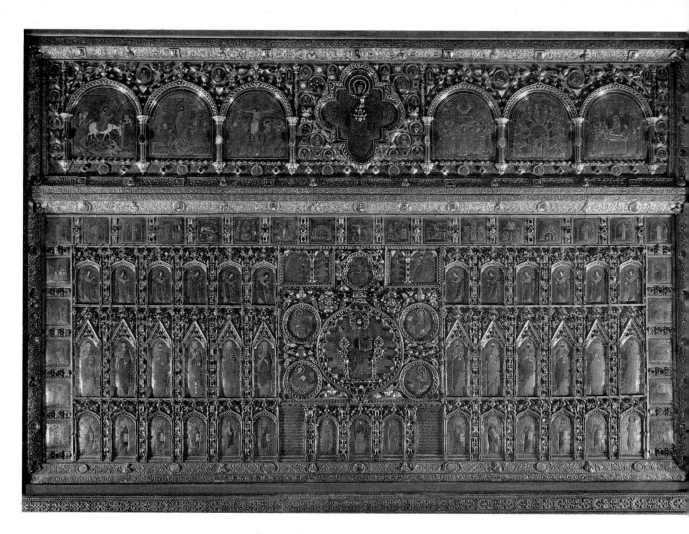

The Pala d'Oro (Golden Altarpiece) – On the altar under which the mortal remains of St. Mark are preserved is a celebrated masterpiece of medieval goldsmithing, the Pala d'Oro. Its original core dates back to 978 when Doge Pietro Orseolo commissioned it from artists in Constantinople. It was rebuilt in 1105 and then in the early 1200s further embellished by the addition of Byzantine gold and enamel pieces which were brought to Venice after the Fourth Crusade of 1204. The materials came from the Orient, but the style and expression are strictly

A detail of the mosaic in the dome over the baptismal font: **An Apostle in the act of baptizing.**

Venetian, for in fact the altar we see today was designed and executed by a Venetian goldsmith, Giampaolo Boninsegna, in 1345. The Pala, measuring 11 by 4.5 feet, has eighty enamel plaques, framed by a myriad of diamonds, emeralds, rubies, and topazes. The scenes illustrated are the lives of Christ, the Virgin, and St. Mark, while the figures represent angels, prophets, evangelists, and Oriental emperors.

The Baptistry – On the following page is a view of the Baptistry which was commissioned by Doge Andrea Dandolo in 1350. The baptismal font in the center was executed by Tiziano Mineo, Desiderio da Firenze, and Francesco Segala in 1545, while the statue of St. John the Baptist was sculpted by Segala in 1575. The tomb of Doge Andrea Dandolo on the right is a 14th century work by the De Sanctis, a family of sculptors. The mosaics on the walls and ceiling by 15th century Venetian masters recount the life of St. John the Baptist and the early years of Christ. On the far wall is a Crucifixion with a portrait of the donor Andrea Dandolo, in the dome above the font, Christ telling the Apostles to preach the Good News, and, on the register below, the Apostle baptizing people from all over the world. In the pendentives are the Four Fathers of the Greek Orthodox church. The mosaic in the dome above the altar shows Christ in Glory, while the figures in the pendentives represent the Four Fathers of the Roman Catholic Church.

61

THE DUCAL PALACE

This remarkable building which has been known as the "Doges' Palace" since the 9th century when the first supreme head of the Venetian state took up residence here, was begun as a Byzantine structure erected over pre-existing Roman walls. The original building commissioned by Doges Angelo and Giustiniano Partecipazio was destroyed by fire and had to be rebuilt. Actually, it was rebuilt several times, but it was not until 1340 that it took on its present appearance as a Venetian Gothic palace.

The name of the architect(s) who designed it has not come down to us, but we have documentary evidence that a certain Filippo Calandario, stonecutter, Pietro Baseio *magister porthus Palacii novii,* and Proto Enrico all worked on the project and we do know that between 1400 and 1424 the façades on the canal and Piazzetta sides were both completed.

Although Milanese and Florentine artists took part in the decoration of the huge palace, most of the decoration in the most elaborate of the medieval styles, the Flamboyant Gothic, was carried out by the members of a famous Venetian family of marble craftsmen, the Bons. Imposing and

majestic, the palace is at the same time the epitome of grace and elegance. The pointed arches of the ground floor arcade create a harmonious base for the dainty second floor loggia which in turn frames the glowing lozenge-patterned façade interspersed with window and balcony accents. The building is crowned by a delicate row of fine crenallation which not only serves as decoration, but, like lace trim on a garment, lightens the effect of the whole. A panoramic view of the façade looking out on the Piazzetta is shown on the preceding centerfold, while the double façade is pictured above.

THE DOGES' PALACE – The **balcony** on the Piazzetta side is by followers of Sansovino. The winged lion with Doge Andrea Gritti is a modern work by U. Bottasso and the figure of Justice on the top was sculpted in the 16th by Alessandro Vittorio.

The Tetrarchs – On the south corner of the basilica (that nearest the Doges' Palace) is a celebrated sculptural group carved out of Egyptian or Syrian porphyry dating from the 4th century and showing four male figures clasped in an embrace. They are believed to represent the Tetrarchs, i.e. emperors at the time of Diocletian.

THE DOGES' PALACE – On the left is another well-known sculptural group practically facing the Teatrarchs on the other side of the Porta della Carta. This expressive work representing the **Judgment of Solomon** has been attributed to the Florentine, Nanni di Bartolo, and followers of the Florentine master, Pietro Lamberti. In the center is the **Porta della Carta** (literally, door of the charters) which got its name from the fact that this is where the scribes who wrote out the documents to be presented to the various offices of the Republic set up their tables. The elaborate Flamboyant Gothic decoration was sculpted in 1348 by Giovanni and Bartolomeo Bon. The figures of Virtues placed in the niches are especially fine works. In the tondo above the three-

part window is a bust of St. Mark and crowning the whole is a statue representing Justice. The figures of Doge Francesco Foscari and the winged lion just above the door were sculpted by Ferrari in 1885 to replace those destroyed in 1797.

On the right is a view of the stupendous 232 foot long façade on the canal side which is adorned with a remarkable Flamboyant Gothic balcony executed by Jacobello and Pier Paolo Dalle Masegne in 1404. The balcony was remodeled in 1575 and the statue of Justice by Alessandro Vittoria was added on the top. In the foreground you can see the **Ponte della Paglia** (literally, Straw Bridge) spanning the Rio di Palazzo which flows by the east side of the palace whose façade was designed by Antonio Rizzo in the 1400s.

THE DOGES' PALACE – The photo above shows the inner **courtyard** of the palace. The bronze well-curbs were sculpted by Niccolò dei Contini in 1556 (foreground) and Alfonso Alberghetti in 1559 (background). The façade on the right, a masterpiece of architectural design created by Antonio Rizzo (1483-1498), is a combination of the Gothic style (the lower storeys) and Renaissance (the upper part). At the far side is the clock façade, a Baroque creation by Bartolomeo Manopola (1614). The figure in the niche in the Foscari Arch by the clock façade represents Francesco Maria Primo della Rovere and was sculpted by a Florentine master, G. Bandini. Below we see the **Staircase of the Giants,** which received its name from the colossal statues of Mars and Neptune on the landing. The staircase was designed by Antonio Rizzo and the statues by Sansovino. Here the doge, as soon as he was elected, was officially crowned before the people and dignitaries assembled below and here too ambassadors and visiting dignitaries waited to be received by the doge. On the right is the **Scala d'Oro** (Golden Staircase) which leads to the doge's private apartments and rooms of the fourth floor. The elaborate gilded stucco decoration which gave it its name was designed by Alessandro Vittoria, while the stairway was built (after a design by Sansovino) between 1523 and 1538. The ceiling frescoes are by G. B. Franco.

THE INTERIOR OF THE DUCAL PALACE

The decoration and embellishment of both the interior and exterior of the Doges' Palace required many years and the collaboration of an army of architects, sculptors, and painters, not to mention the skilled craftsmen such as marble and stonecutters, woodworkers, and masters in the arts of stuccoing and gilding. Starting from the 15th century, name artists were summoned from all over Italy to work on the project, among them Gentile da Fabriano and Pisanello who worked on the painting cycles in the Sala del Maggior Consiglio. In the 16th century the palace must have been truly breathtaking if you think that by the 1570s the Bellinis, the Vivarinis, Carpaccio, Titian, Paolo Veronese, and Tintoretto had completed their paintings in the other rooms of the palace.

Then on May 11, 1574 and December 20, 1577 disaster struck. On each of these occasions fire broke out, destroying the various Sala del Collegio, Sala del Senato, and completely gutting the upper floors of the building on the Piazzetta and canal sides.

Detail of the **Sala Grimani (Grimani Room)**.

Detail of the **Sala delle Quattro Porte (Room of the Four Doors)**.

In one fell swoop all of the works by the celebrated artists who had collaborated on the palace decoration, as well as the fittings and furniture, were wiped away. As a result, it was decided to restore as much as possible and to rebuild respecting the original Gothic structure. Antonio da Ponte who was appointed to supervise the project soon saw to it that the architecture was reconstructed and that the Sala del Maggior Consiglio and the Sala dello Scrutinio were restored and fitted with new paintings, furnishings, and objets d'art. Unfortunately, due to the political events following the occupation of Venice by Napoleon's troops in 1797, not all of these furnishings have come down to us. The Venetians, exasperated and anxious to cancel all symbols and signs of the past, stormed the palace and proceeded to destroy anything they could lay their hands on. During the French, and later Austrian, occupation, the palace was taken over for use as government offices, which hardly proved of benefit for the physical condition of the building. In fact, the deterioration was so great that it was necessary to carry out a complete restoration in 1874. More recently, the Sopraintendenza ai Monumenti (the Italian state agency in charge of monuments) has done a praiseworthy job of restoring and keeping the palace in a perfect state of conservation.

The Painting Gallery: the *Lion of St. Mark's* by Carpaccio (detail).

THE DOGES' PALACE – This is the **Anticollegio,** that is the antechamber where magistrates and illustrious guests waited to be received by the doge. The elaborate stucco decoration is by Alessandro Vittoria and the allegorical paintings by Francesco Montemezzano. Over the door are sculptures by Vittoria. The painting above the door representing Pallas and Mars is by J. Tintoretto, while the one on the right of the Rape of Europa is by Paolo Veronese.

THE DOGES' PALACE – This is the **Sala del Collegio** designed by Palladio in 1573 where the College, or Council, composed of the most important dignitaries of the Republic, held their meetings presided over by the Doge. Here the Council deliberated affairs of state and received foreign ambassadors. The ceiling contains masterpieces painted by Paolo Veronese. On the walls are fine works by Domenico and Jacopo Tintoretto.

THE DOGES' PALACE – This is the **Sala del Senato,** or Senate Hall, where the senators, presided over by the doge, held their meetings. The subjects of the paintings on the walls and ceilings all have to do with the glorification of divine favor towards the Republic. The room was remodeled by Antonio da Ponte. The impressive gilded stucco ceiling (by Cristoforo

Sorte) contains a masterpiece by Tintoretto representing the Triumph of Venice with mythological figures. The paintings in the ovals are by Dolabella. On the wall behind the raised platform is a symbolic painting showing the Doge adoring the dead Christ by Jacopo Tintoretto. On the wall to the left (by the clock) are paintings by Jacopo Palma the Younger.

THE DOGES' PALACE – This is the **Sala del Consiglio dei Dieci** (Room of the Council of Ten) where the much feared magistrates in charge of security of state held their trials for political crimes against the Republic. The subjects of the paintings decorating the room refer to the characteristics that were supposed to inspire the conduct of the members of the Council. On the left wall, Pope Alexander III, Frederick Redbeard, and Doge Ziani by Francesco Leandro da Ponte, on the right wall, the Adoration of the Magi by Alienese, and, on the ceiling, Jupiter striking down the Vices (facing page, above), a 19th century copy of Paolo Veronese's original now in the Louvre.

On the right: this is the **Sala della Bussola** (literally, the Compass Room). The odd double door in the foreground, nicknamed *bussola,* or compass, gave the room its name. On the right wall is a painting by Alienese representing Carmagnola conquering Bergamo and on the ceiling is another copy of a Veronese (the original is in the Louvre) showing St. Mark crowning the Theological Virtues.

THE DOGES' PALACE – On an easel in the **Sala degli Scudieri** (Squires' Room) is one of Tiepolo's finest works showing Neptune offering the gifts of the sea to Venice.

THE DOGES' PALACE – This is the **Sala dei Tre Capi del Consiglio dei Dieci** (Room of the Three Heads of the Council of Ten). On the ceiling is a fine painting by G. B. Zelotti showing the Victory of Virtue over Vice. The elaborate fireplace was designed by Sansovino and built by his pupils, Pietro Grazioli da Salò and Danese Cattaneo. The room was the headquarters for the magistrates in charge of correspondence and scheduled Council meetings.

THE DOGES' PALACE – This is the **Sala d'Armi** (Weapons Room), that is the Armory of the Council of Ten. In it are exhibited arms and armor of great renown. This collection of 15th and 16th century pieces is truly unique, as it is made up of weapons really used to defend the palace (plus parade and jousting arms) and not the usual museum hodgepodge of pieces randomly acquired here and there. In addition, the collection includes relics and documents relating to the victories of the Republic. By 1317 the Doges' Palace already had its own armory, but then in 1532 this room was selected as the new arsenal. Although numerous pieces were dispersed, especially during the French looting of 1797, the collection presently totals about 2000 objects.

THE DOGES' PALACE – This is the **Sala del Maggior Consiglio** (Hall of the Greater Council) in which the supreme Venetian magistrates exerted power. The room measures 176 feet long, 82 feet wide, and 51 feet high. Destroyed by fire in 1557, it was rebuilt by Antonio da Ponte and embellished with paintings whose iconography involving the glorification of the Venetian Republic, was drawn up by Girolamo de' Bardi, a Florentine scholar, and F. Sansovino, a Venetian historian. On the ceiling is a large panel by Jacopo Tintoretto representing Venice amidst the gods receiving homage from her subjects and, above the raised platform, a grandiose canvas by Tintoretto, known as Paradise.

On the facing page is the **Sala dello Scrutinio** (Voting Room) rebuilt by Antonio da Ponte after the fire of 1577. The iconography of the paintings involving the glorification of the Venetian Republic on the high seas was created by Girolamo de' Bardi. The Arch of Triumph against the far wall was built by A. Tirali in 1694 to honor Doge Francesco Morosini for his conquest of Peloponnesus. On the righthand wall are the Battle of Lepanto by A. Vicentino and the Victory of the Dardanelles by Liberi.

THE DOGES' PALACE: in the photo above, the entrance to the **Prigioni Nuove (New Prison)**; below, a cell in the **pozzi** (dungeons). The prison is reached by way of the Doges' Palace, passing inside the Bridge of Sighs.

The Bridge of Sighs – Above is the celebrated bridge which, passing over the Rio di Palazzo, connects the Doges' Palace to the prisons. It was built in 1599 by Antonio Contino. Prisoners, on their way to appear before the judges, would cross it and look through the lattice-work windows, probably uttering sighs of sadness for their lost freedom.

Above: gondolas moored between the Rio di Palazzo and the Rio del Vin. Alongside the Doges' Palace is the old prison built between 1589 and 1614 which in turn is next to the 15th century **Palazzo Dandolo,** now part of the exclusive Danieli Hotel.

Right: a view of the **Riva degli Schiavoni,** one of the nicest places to walk in Venice. It was named after the Dalmation merchants from Slavonia who moored their trading ships here. In the foreground, the rooftops of the Doges' Palace, in the background the peaceful Isle of San Pietro. The church of St. Peter's on the island was once the cathedral of Venice.

A STROLL THROUGH VENICE

A stroll along the Grand Canal and around Piazza San Marco means that you have been introduced to the Queen of the Adriatic, but you do not as yet know her very well. If you really want to get to know her, you must wander about her *calli, rii, campi,* and *campielli,* without being afraid of losing your way. Only by walking up and down the narrow streets can you discover, sestiere by sestiere, all her charms, artistic and otherwise, the splendor of her palaces and churches, and the quaintness of her neighborhoods. Only by walking can you notice the remarkable effects of light reflect-

ing on the water and buildings and the bright colors of the clothes-lines, bird cages, and flower pots hanging from the houses. Above all, only by walking, can you get to know the Venetians, famous for their hospitality and kindness, so prompt to help you find your way if you are lost (whatever your native tongue), and so ready to make you feel at ease. Only in this way can you really say you know Venice and only by living such an experience can you take away indelible memories of the city to savor when you have returned to your home town and your more mundane everyday existence.

In the Sestiere (quarter) of Castello is the **Campo Santa Maria Formosa** with the church of the same name we see pictured above. The church was founded in the 7th century on the spot where the Virgin had appeared as a stately matron and thus its name (*formosa,* in fact, means stately). Remodeled by Mauro Coducci in 1492, the building has two 16th century façades, one on the square side (erected in 1542) and one on the canal side (erected in 1604). The busts on the square façade are of members of the Cappello family who sponsored the project. The figures on the very top represent the Virgin and Virtues and were sculpted in the 1700s.

The Dominican church of **San Giovanni e Paolo,** begun in 1246 and finished in 1430, is a fine example of Venetian Gothic architecture. The Pantheon of Venice, it contains the tombs of several well-known Venetians who were given burial inside it. On the unfinished brick façade is an exquisite portal attributed to Antonio Gambello which is a marvelous combination of two different styles, Gothic and Renaissance.

The famous **equestrian statue of Bartolomeo Colleoni** by the Florentine master Andrea del Verrocchio (photo left on the facing page) stands in the Campo San Giovanni e Paolo in the Sestiere di Castello. The monument designed by Verrocchio was cast by Alessandro Leopardi who is also responsible for the fine base.

On the Rio dei Mendicanti (Beggars' Canal) side of the Campo San Giovanni e Paolo is the **Scuola Grande di San Marco,** now the city hospital, a Renaissance masterpiece put up by Pietro Lombardo and Mauro Coducci between 1485 and 1495. The façade sculptures are by Bartolomeo Bon and T. Lombardo.

The photo on the left shows the monumental entrance to the **Arsenal,** once the shipyard of the *"Repubblica di San Marco."* The triumphal arch entranceway is a Renaissance work designed by Antonio Gambello in 1460. On either side are marble lions which came to Venice as part of the war booty carried off by Admiral Francesco Morosini. Above: the **Rio San Iseppo** not far from the Castello Gardens. Below: the **Ponte Nuovo (New Bridge)** which crosses the Rio San Severo

Above is the **church of San Zaccaria** on the campo of the same name in the Sestiere di Castello. Originally built in the 10th century, it was remodeled between 1470 and 1500 by Antonio Gambello and Mauro Coducci who are also responsible for the magnificent façade, a masterpiece of the Venetian Renaissance style. The statue of St. Zacheriah above the portal is by Alessandro Vittoria. On either side of the portal are figures of prophets within fine Renaissance frames. Inside, in the Chapel of San Tarasio, are three splendid 15th century altarpieces.

Above: **Campo di Santi Filippo e Giacomo;**
below: **Campo San Bartolomeo.**

Above: **Campo di Santi Filippo e Giacomo;**
below: **the Ruga degli Orefici.**

This curious Lombard spiral staircase designed in the 16th century by Giovanni Candi is in the courtyard of the Palazzo Contarini Dal Bovolo.

On the left is a photo of the **church of San Giacomo di Rialto,** believed to be the oldest in Venice, which was rebuilt in the 11th-12th centuries. The rather odd-looking façade has a fine Gothic portico. Below the Gothic relief representing the Virgin and child on the bell-tower is a clock constructed in 1410.

Below: The **Rio San Moisè** passes the church of the same name (facing page) on its way to emptying into the Grand Canal between the Palazzo Tiepolo and the Palazzo Treves dei Bonfili.

The **church of San Moisè** (facing page) was originally built in the 8th century in honor of St. Vittore. Then, in the 10th century, its reconstruction was sponsored by a certain Moisè who gave it the name of his name saint. The façade in an extremely elaborate Baroque style was erected by Tremignon and Meyring in 1688. Inside, is the tomb (dated 1729) of Giovanni Law who is famous for having introduced paper money into the banking system, and fine works by Palma the Younger and Tintoretto.

Two aerial views of the picturesque rooftops of Venice. In the photo above
we can make out the church of San Giovanni e Paolo and the Scuola Grande
di San Marco in the background.

A monument to Niccolò Tommaseo by Francesco Barzaghi (1882) stands in the middle of the huge **Campo Santo Stefano.** Here we see only a section of the campo which contains a number of important monuments such as the churches of San Vitale and Santo Stefano and the Franchetti, Pisani, and Loredan palaces. Once public festivals were held here.

The **Rio del Malpaga** is a charming canal which flows into the Grand Canal.

The **Rio San Vio** is the waterway connecting the Grand and Giudecca canals.

The photo on the upper left of the preceding page shows the **church of San Barnaba,** designed in 1749 by Lorenzo Boschetti, located in the Sestiere di Dorsoduro. It has a neo-Classical façade with Corinthian columns and a tympanum over the portal. The brick belltower is in the Romanesque style. Inside is one of Paolo Veronese's masterpieces, a painting of the Holy Family.

Not far from the Campo San Trovaso (SS. Gervasio e Protasio) on the canal of San Trovaso (in the Sestiere di Dorsoduro) is a shipyard where gondolas are built and repaired. Venice was once full of these picturesque **squeri** (yards) and this typical example shows us what the poorer people's wood and cement houses must have once looked like. In the background is the church of San Trovaso which was founded in the 11th century and rebuilt in 1584 in the Palladian style.

Above: a view of the picturesque **Rio di San Barnaba** which flows by Ca' Rezzonico.

The Church of Santa Maria Gloriosa dei Frari – This remarkable church is not far from the Ca' Granda in the Sestiere di San Polo. Ranking after St. Mark's as the most important Venetian Gothic structure in Venice, the church contains tombs of famous Venetians (as does the church of San Giovanni e Paolo) and important works of art. Attributed to an architect-monk, Fra Scipione Bon, it was commissioned by a religious order, the Frati Minori di San Francesco, and erected between 1340 and 1443. The unadorn yet impressive brick façade is decorated with sculptures over the portal by Alessandro Vittoria and Bartolomeo Bon.

The interior of the church of Santa Maria Gloriosa conveys an impression of great stateliness. Twelve round columns crossed by tierods set off the nave from the aisles. Above are simple brick ribbed vaults whose pointed arches heighten the effect of space. The exquisite choir in the center contains fine sculptures by Bartolomeo Bon and Pietro Lombardo.

On the right is a photo of Titian's celebrated masterpiece, the **Assumption,** which is one of the highlights of the church. The painting measures 21 by 17 feet.

The church of San Rocco, begun in 1489 and only completed in the 18th century, contains the relics of the French saint, St. Roch, who dedicated his life to taking care of the sick and helpless. The façade designed by Maccaruzzi between 1765 and 1771 was inspired by the façade of the nearby Scuola di San Rocco designed by Mauro Coducci. In the portal lunette is a bronze reproduction executed by G. Marchiori of the marble relief which once adorned this space (it represents St. Roch being carried to heaven by angels). The same artist is also responsible for the statues of Sts. Pietro Orseolo and Gherardo Safredo in the niches on either side of the portal. On the second level is a marble relief showing St. Roch assisting the sick with statues of saints on either side.

On the right is a section of the huge **Campo San Polo** (or San Paolo in Italian) which contains the church of the same name as well as a number of outstanding palaces such as Palazzo Tiepolo, Palazzo Donà, and Palazzo Corner-Mocenigo. In this campo, the largest in Venice, numerous public spectacles from fairs to meetings, bullfights, and military parades were held.

Below is the **Canale di Cannaregio,** one of the main waterways connecting the Grand Canal and the lagoon.

Above left is a charming view of the **Punta della Dogana** with the domes of the church of Santa Maria della Salute visible in the background.

Below is a photo of the **church of San Giorgio Maggiore** with its glowing white Palladian façade and the old Benedictine monastery on the Isle of San Giorgio Maggiore, (they now belong to a cultural institute, the Cini Foundation). The church was designed by Andrea Palladio and erected between 1565 and 1610. The belltower was erected in 1791 by the Bolognese architect Benedetto Buratti to replace the original which collapsed in 1773.

Below is the heavily-trafficked **Giudecca Canal,** the site of busy shipyards and factories, as seen from the Isle of San Giorgio Maggiore. There are two theories regarding the origin of the name Giudecca. One is that the Jews (*giudei*) were once confined to this neighborhood, whereas the second would have it that Giudecca comes from *Zudega* (the judged ones) due to the fact that rebel nobles were banished here in the 9th century.

A wide-angle view of the final stretch of the Giudecca canal. In the center are the domes of the Church of Santa Maria della Salute, Baldassarre Longhena's 17th century masterpiece. On the right is the elegant building known as the Dogana da Mar. On the huge gilded globe surmounting it is a weathervane in the form of a statue of Fortune.

The pictures on these pages show **floods** in Venice. This is a rather frequent occurrence in the city as high tides in fall and winter often cause flooding.

On the upper left: the **La Fenice Theater,** Venice's most important, which was built at the end of the 18th century. Below, the window display of a Venetian restaurant featuring the city's seafood specialties of fish and shellfish dishes. On this page, two nighttime views of the city: **Piazza San Marco** and the **Belltower.**

The Regata Storica —
The custom of holding *regate* (boat races) in Venice, while rooted in the past, is still very much alive today. Of all the *regate,* the best known and most spectacular —and judging from participation, the most popular— is the *Regata Storica* (historic boat race) which is held the first Sunday of September. The idea of holding a race of this kind has always been attributed to Doge Giovanni Soranzo, in 1315, though the *regata* as we see it today dates from a personal initiative of Mayor Filippo Grimani of 1896. The spectacle consists of an immense parade down the Grand Canal, the participants dressed in traditional costume, which is followed by a race contended by the best oarsmen in Venice. The boats, laden with ornaments and coats of arms, twice circle the Grand Canal; the local dignitaries and crowds lining the canalbanks can enjoy the colorful pageant before the start of the actual boat race.

117

THE ENVIRONS OF VENICE

We shall now turn to the group of splendid islands which are like gem stones scattered about the lagoon, the most precious of which is Venice. There are all kinds, ranging in size from tiny uninhabited islets to good-sized islands, now sleepy fishing villages but once thriving cities. A trip to Torcello, Burano, Murano is a must for those who desire to really know Venice.

These island cities are fascinating not only for the art treasures they possess, but also for their hauntingly beautiful landscapes in an atmosphere of magical silence—and this is not all the lagoon has to offer. We must not forget the local handicrafts; glassmaking, lacemaking, and copper crafting are some of the typical products of the local artisans.

The Lido of Venice – The Lido is actually an elongated island about a mile from Venice. Once the city's natural defense, it is now a world famous resort. Its reputation rests on its well-equipped hotels and excellent tourist accommodations, its fine sandy beach, and the cultural, artistic, and sporting events held here throughout the year.

The island of Murano: Originally called Amurianum, present-day Murano is one of the biggest islands in the Venetian lagoon. Like Venice, it is composed of numerous little islands crisscrossed by canals with bridges, *fondamenta,* and *calli.* Its origins are believed to go back to the 10th century, after which time it achieved self-government and was granted the right to have its own nobility and the privilege of minting the so-called *"oselle"* (that is, the souvenir coins to mark the election of the doges of Venice). A flourishing industrial center favored by the Republic of Venice, it reached the height of splendor in the 16th century, mainly due to its burgeoning glassblowing industry.

Above: an aerial view of the island of Murano. Right: the **Grand Canal of Murano** which bisects the whole island. A famous boat race is held every year on this canal.

Above: the apse of the **Basilica of Santa Maria e Donato,** a 12th century Venetian Byzantine church. The interior of the church is adorned with splendid mosaics. Especially noteworthy is a grandiose Virgin in the semi-dome of the apse. Murano is renowned for its **glass-blowing,** an art which dates back to 1289 in the city. It flourished throughout the 15th and 16th centuries and, after a period of decline, revived in the 18th due to the introduction of new techniques. During the 19th century it again went into decline, but it is now enjoying an even bigger revival. In the upper righthand photo of the facing page is a craftsman at work. Below are some typical examples of the glassblower's art.

The island of Burano: Burano was founded in the 5th century by the inhabitants of Altinum who were fleeing Attila's Huns. Interestingly enough, the present-day population retains something of their long-ago origin in the characteristic cadence of their dialect which recalls the pronounciation of the Altinate people. One of the most interesting sights on the island is the 16th century church of San Martino. Inside the single aisle church, which is in the shape of a Latin cross and which has a fine vaulted ceiling, are several noteworthy works of art, including a grandiose Crucifixion painted by G. B. Tiepolo in 1725. Burano's best-known native son is the composer Buranello (1703-1785).

The photo above shows an aerial view of Burano. Above right: a canal in Burano lined with picturesque brightly-painted houses. Below left: **Burano lacemaking.** The island of Burano is celebrated for its laces and embroidery which have been a major source of the economic prosperity of its inhabitants. The hand-crafted laces are renowned worldover for the intricacy and skillfulness of the needlework involved in creating these delicate masterpieces. Already known by the 15th century, Burano lacework found a staunch sponsor in the Medici queen of France, Caterina, herself a skilled embroiderer, in the 1500s. Caterina patronized the Italian lacemakers who enriched the art by adding new and evermore complicated stitches to those already in existence. On the right is the **belltower** of the church of San Martino.

The island of Torcello: Torcello, like Burano, was founded between the 5th and 6th centuries by people fleeing the Huns and Longobards who had overrun Altinum, and, in fact, its original name was Nuova Altino (New Altinum). Torcello (literally, little tower), on the other hand, derives from an old tower, probably a watchtower for guards posted as lookouts. Under the Byzantine emperors in the 7th century, it achieved bishopric status and was so successful as a trading center that it quickly became one of the major lagoon cities, boasting a population of 20,000. Thereafter, with the rise of Venice, Torcello started to decline and within a short time—made even shorter by the spread of the marshlands—the once prosperous city was reduced to practically a ghost town. Today, Torcello is a tiny village inhabited mainly by fishermen and, due to its enormous historical and artistic importance, a constant drawing-card for sightseers and scholars.

In the photo below is the **Devil's Bridge.**

Photo above right: on the left we see the most important monument on the island of Torcello, the **cathedral of Santa Maria Assunta,** and on the right the remarkable church of Santa Fosca. Although Santa Maria was founded in 639, it underwent modifications in 864 and 1008 and is now prevalently Byzantine in appearance. The imposing belltower was erected in the 11th century. The single aisle basilican interior contains marvelous mosaics, the most striking of which is the grandiose Last Judgment on the inner façade wall, dating from the 12th century. The Ravennate-style **church of Santa Fosca,** rebuilt in the 11th century, has a distinctive exterior composed of a porch sustained by marble columns and brick pillars, and an octagonal apse. The Greek cross interior is midway between a square and circular shape, as the plans to add on a dome were never carried out. As you can tell from this brief description, Santa Fosca is extremely interesting from an architectural standpoint. Below right is a detail of the village of Torcello and the canal leading from the lagoon up to it.

INDEX